LET'S LOOK AT THE SKY: THE STARS

The name of Patrick Moore is synonymous with night skies, constellations, Apollo Moon shots, and BBC radio and television broadcasting.

In LET'S LOOK AT THE SKY: THE STARS Patrick Moore covers such topics as The Stars at Night; Stories from the Sky; Finding Your Way Around The Sky; the Life and Death of a Star; How Did the Universe Begin. This book is profusely illustrated with 'easy-to-follow' diagrams and there are lots of experiments for you to do as you discover an absorbing new world.

Also by Patrick Moore

THE ASTRONOMY QUIZ BOOK
LET'S LOOK AT THE SKY: THE PLANETS

and published by CAROUSEL BOOKS

Patrick Moore

LET'S LOOK AT THE SKY: THE STARS

Illustrated by Lawrence Clarke
and Jocelyn Knox

Consultant editor: Anne Wood

TRANSWORLD PUBLISHERS LTD

LET'S LOOK AT THE SKY: THE STARS

A CAROUSEL BOOK 0 552 54082 X

First published in Great Britain 1975

PRINTING HISTORY
Carousel edition published 1975

Carousel books are published by Transworld
Publishers Ltd.,
Cavendish House, 57–59 Uxbridge Road,
Ealing, London, W.5.

Made and printed in Great Britain by
Cox & Wyman Ltd., London, Reading and Fakenham

CONTENTS

THE STARS AT NIGHT

IN *Let's Look At The Sky: The Planets* we were talking about the Sun, the Moon and the planets. Now it is time to look at the stars. You cannot see stars in the daytime, because the Sun makes the sky too bright, but as soon as the Sun sets the stars begin to come out.

The Earth on which we live is a planet – that is to say a large ball, moving round the Sun and taking one year to make a full journey. There are eight other planets, of which the brightest are Venus, Mars, Jupiter and Saturn. With the naked eye (that is to say, without using binoculars or a telescope) the planets look like stars, but they are really quite different. Like the Moon, they have no light of their own, and shine only because they are being lit up by the Sun. If the Sun suddenly went out, the Moon and planets would disappear too, but luckily this cannot possibly happen! The Sun's family makes up what we call the Solar System.

The Sun itself is a star. This is not easy to believe at first, because the Sun looks so brilliant while the stars are tiny dots of light; but it is true. Some of the stars which you can see on any clear night are much hotter and more powerful than the Sun, and seem fainter only because they are so much further away from us. If the Sun were taken out to the distance of any of the stars, it too would look like a speck of light.

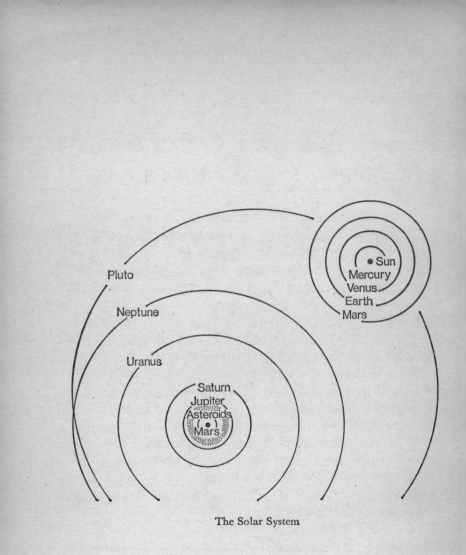

The Solar System

If you make a model in which the distance between the Earth and the Sun is scaled down to 2·5 cm, as shown here, how far away will the nearest star be? The answer is – over six kilometres! You can see, then, that the stars are very distant indeed.

SUN   EARTH   Nearest star 6 kilometers

The sky seems to turn round the Earth once in 24 hours, not because it is really doing so, but because the Earth itself is spinning. If you stand in the middle of a room and turn round and round very quickly, the room will appear to move, and if you spin fast enough you will become dizzy; but the room itself stays still. It is the same with the sky. We live on a spinning world; the Sun, the Moon, the planets and the stars all seem to move round us, which is why people who lived hundreds of years ago thought that the Earth must lie in the middle of the whole universe.

There is, however, one great difference between the movements of the planets and the movements of the stars. The planets wander about the sky, but the stars do not. The stars always keep in the same patterns, and do not change, so that they look the same now as they did in the time of Jesus Christ. The patterns are called *constellations*, and have been given names such as the Great Bear, the Swan and the Eagle.

Of these groups or constellations, perhaps the best known is the Great Bear; some people call it the Plough, while in America it is called the Big Dipper. From England you can always see it whenever the sky is dark and clear, and you will be able to find it easily. The diagram given here shows its shape. The pattern is always the same, and there is nothing else like it in the sky.

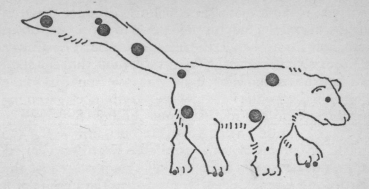

Yet the stars are not really standing still in space; they are moving about very quickly, in all sorts of directions. They seem to keep in the same positions because they are so far away from us. The best way to show this is to go outdoors at a time when an aircraft is flying overhead, and to see how slowly the aircraft seems to crawl against the clouds above it. Now take a stone, and throw it upward. The stone will seem to move quickly against the clouds; but it is not moving nearly so fast as the aircraft.

The further away a moving body is, the slower it seems to go. The stars are so far away that they seem to 'stop', and keep in the same positions compared with each other. It is true that astronomers using special instruments can measure the movements of the stars; but these movements are so slight that for the moment we can ignore them.

As the Earth spins, and the sky moves, the stars travel round 'all together', just as the specks of mud on a football will do when you spin the football. It is only the Sun, Moon and planets, which are so much closer to us, which show noticeable movements of their own, and wander from one constellation to another.

There is one star in the sky which seems to keep in almost the same place all the time. This is the Pole Star, which you can find because it is lined up with two of the stars of the Great Bear. The Earth's axis of rotation points to a position very close to the Pole Star, and so the Pole Star keeps due north, with everything else seeming to move round it. From England, the Pole Star is quite high up, because England is in the northern part of the Earth; but if you go to Australia or New Zealand you will never see it all – because it does not rise above the horizon. The south pole star is very faint, and not easy to find unless you know just where to look for it. From Europe you will never see it at all.

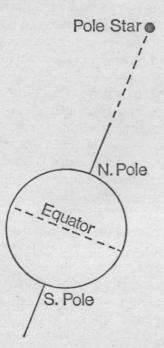

2

HOW FAR ARE THE STARS

IF you set out to walk two kilometres – say from your home to the nearest town, or to the house of a friend – you will feel quite tired by the time you arrive. Two kilometres seem a long way. Yet to an astronomer it is not far; and even the Sun is 150 million kilometres away. To walk a distance equal to that between the Earth and the Sun would take you over three thousand years, even if you never stopped at all, and the stars are much further away still.

Astronomers have found a way of measuring the distances to the stars, and the method is worth explaining, because you can make a simple experiment to show how it works. Close one eye, and hold out a finger at arm's-length, as the girl in the picture is doing. Line up your finger with something in the distance, such as a tree. Now, without moving your head or your finger, close your first eye and open the other. You will find that your finger is no longer lined up with the tree, because you are looking from a different direction; your two eyes are not in the same place.

In the next diagram I have shown what has happened. From Eye No.1, your finger will be lined up with the tree; when you use Eye No.2, your finger will appear in the position marked X. If you know the distance between your eyes, and you know how much your finger seems to have shifted, you can draw the whole diagram to scale, and measure the distance between your finger and your face.

If you line your finger up with the tree, then look at it with one eye, then the other eye, your finger will appear to have moved.

The Earth moves round the Sun in a period of one year, so that in six months it travels from one side of the

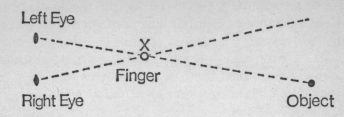

Sun to the other, as shown in the next diagram. The star marked S is much closer than the stars in the background. First, we measure the star's position in January; when we measure it again six months later, in June, the star will seem to have moved, just as your finger seemed to move against the tree. Again we can draw the whole diagram, and measure the distance of the star S.

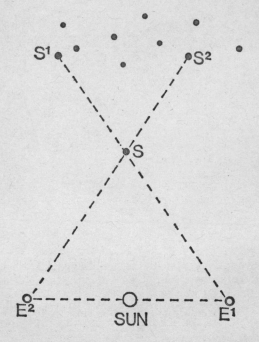

Of course, things are not nearly so easy as might be thought from these pictures. The star S will move only very slightly, and we must also remember that the Sun itself is moving, taking the Earth along with it; but by now many stars have had their distances measured in this way, which is known as *the method of parallax*.

The stick and the tree are not really as close as they seem from this angle.

Because the stars are not all at the same distance from us, the constellation patterns do not mean very much. The Great Bear is a good case of this. Of the two stars in the Bear's tail, one is more than twice as far away from us as the other; they simply happen to lie in much the same direction as seen from Earth, so that they appear side by side in the sky. Again you can carry out an easy experiment. Put a stick upright in the ground, and then walk some distance from it, bending down until the stick seems to be lined up beside a tree at the far end of the garden. The stick and the tree are not really close together; they only appear to be so.

This is something that people of long ago did not know. They thought that the stars were at the same distance from us, and were fixed on to a solid sky! They had no idea that each star is a sun.

All the stars, apart from our Sun, are so far away that it would be awkward to give their distances in kilometres, because the kilometre is too short a unit – just as nobody would give the distance between London and Glasgow in centimetres. Astronomers use a different unit, known as a light-year.

Light takes a definite time to travel. If you switch on a torch in a dark room, it takes time for the light to go from the torch-bulb to the far wall; but you cannot measure the time taken, because light moves so quickly that it can go from the Earth to the Moon in less than one and a half seconds. In a year, a ray of light can travel almost ninety-six hundred thousand million kilometres and this is the astronomer's 'light-year'. A light-year, then, is a measure of distance, not of time. If you want to change light-years into kilometres, all you have to do is to multiply by six million million.

It takes light eight and a half minutes to reach us from

the Sun, so that when you look at the Sun you are seeing it as it used to be eight and a half minutes ago. The nearest star is over four light-years away. Look at the Pole Star, and you are seeing it as it used to be about seven hundred years ago, at the time of the Crusades. If the Pole Star suddenly stopped shining, it would be another seven hundred years before we could know that anything had happened to it. When we look outside the Sun's family or Solar System, our view of everything in the sky must always be very out of date. We cannot (like Dr. Who!) travel in time; but when we see the stars, we are at least looking backwards through time.

3

STORIES FROM THE SKY

MANY of the constellations are named after the gods and heroes of the old stories which go back long before the time of Jesus Christ. There are plenty of these stories; so let me retell some of them – beginning with the adventure of the princess and the sea-monster.

The princess was named Andromeda. Her father, King Cepheus, was ruler of a large island; her mother, Queen Cassiopeia, was very proud of Andromeda's beauty. Unfortunately, she was heard to say that Andromeda was more beautiful than the 'sea-nymphs', lovely girls who lived in the sea and were the daughters of the powerful sea-god Neptune. Neptune was so angry about this that he sent a monster to attack the kingdom. The monster caused great damage; houses and farms were ruined, people were killed, and the King and Queen were at their wits' end.

What was to be done? They found that the only way to save the country was to chain their daughter, Princess Andromeda, to a rock on the sea-shore, where she would be eaten by the monster. Of course they had no wish to do this, but there seemed to be no help for it. So Andromeda was tied to the rock, and left there to wait for the monster.

The princess was terribly frightened, and thought that nobody would be able to come to her help, but suddenly she saw a young man flying through the air towards her. His name was Perseus, and he was the son of the king of a far-away country. Perseus was wearing some wonderful shoes which had wings on them; they had been loaned to him by Mercury, one of the gods (after whom the planet Mercury is named). Perseus had just killed a dreadful creature named Medusa, who had the body and head of a woman, but whose hair was made up of live snakes which hissed and spat. Perscus had cut off Medusa's head, and was now carrying it wrapped up in a bag made of a goat's skin. He had to cover the head, because Medusa was so terrible that nobody could look at her without being turned into stone.

Perseus flew down beside Andromeda, and found out what was happening. He waited until the monster came towards him out of the sea, and then he uncovered Medusa's head. At once the monster stopped; it was changed into a huge stone, and could do no more harm. Perseus untied Andromeda, and took her back to the King and Queen, who were overjoyed to see her safe and well. The story had a happy ending; Perseus married Andromeda, and they spent the rest of their long lives together. When they died, they were made into gods and were put into the sky, where you can still see them. King Cepheus and Queen Cassiopeia are there as well, and even the sea-monster has been remembered, though on

CASSIOPEIA

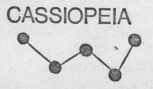

some star-maps the monster has been turned into a harmless whale.

Of these constellations, Cassiopeia is the easiest to find; the stars make up a pattern which looks rather like a W or M, as shown here, and it is not easy to see how the old story-tellers could make it into the figure of a woman. But this does not matter; very few of the constellations look anything like the people or things after which they are named, and the stories are none the less interesting because of this.

Another tale with a happy ending is that of Orion, who was said to be a great huntsman. He was so big and strong that he believed he could kill any animal on earth; but he was himself killed by a scorpion, which crawled out of a hole in the ground and stung him in the foot. The gods took pity on him, bringing him back to life and placing him in the sky. Orion is one of the most brilliant of all the constellations, and you can see him in the evening sky all through winter and early spring. He has two particularly bright stars, Betelgeux in his shoulder and Rigel in his foot.

The scorpion is in the sky, too, with its heart marked by the very red Antares; but to make sure that the scorpion can do Orion no further harm, it has been put as far away from Orion as it could possibly be. You will never see Orion and the scorpion above the horizon at the same time!

Not far from Orion is another bright constellation, known as the Twins. The two most brilliant stars, Castor and Pollux, also have a story. According to the tale, Castor and Pollux were twin brothers who were very fond of each other, and always stayed together, but Pollux was immortal – that is to say, he could never die – while Castor was not. When Castor was killed, Pollux was so sad that he asked to be allowed to share his immortality with his brother. So Castor was brought back to life, and both he and Pollux were taken up into the sky to shine down side by side.

During summer evenings you will be able to see a small group of stars which we call the Dolphin. The stars themselves are not bright, but they are so close together that they are easy to find. The story about them begins with Arion, who was so great a musician than when he began singing even the animals and birds stopped to listen to him. Once he took part in a competiton, and of course he won all the prizes. After the end of the competition he went on board ship to sail home, but the sailors knew that he was bringing gold and jewels with him, so they made up their minds to kill Arion and steal his prizes.

As soon as they were out of sight of land, the sailors took hold of Arion and threw him into the sea. There they left him, sure that he would drown. But while Arion was swimming, a dolphin came up to him; Arion climbed on to the dolphin's back, and was taken safely to the shore. When the sailors reached home, they found Arion waiting for them – together with the king's soldiers, who put the sailors in prison and gave Arion's gold back to him. Because the dolphin had been so friendly, it was given a place in the sky when it died.

These are only a few of the old tales. They are always worth re-telling, and it is said that the sky is a complete picture-book which anyone can learn how to read.

4
FINDING YOUR WAY AROUND
THE SKY

HOW many stars can you see on a dark night? You may think that the answer is 'millions', but this is not true. You can never see more than about three thousand stars without using binoculars or a telescope, and not many of these are really bright.

It is not hard to learn your way around the sky, and to pick out the most important constellations. If you practise for a few evenings, you will soon find that you are starting to learn the patterns. The bright constellations can be used as 'signposts'; one group of stars will show the way to the next, and of course the constellations never change. When I started to look at the night sky, I made up my mind to recognize and learn one new constellation on every clear night; before long I had come to know them well.

Let us begin with the Great Bear, partly because it is so easy to find and partly because it never sets over the British Isles (or the northern part of the United States of America). This is because it is so near the north pole of the sky. Like everything else, it seems to circle round the Pole Star, because the Earth is spinning; but as you can see from the diagram, it never drops below the horizon, and you can always see it whenever the sky is dark and clear. The two end stars, which show the way to the Pole Star, are called the Pointers.

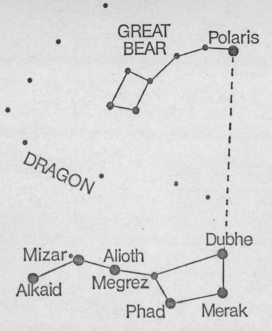

Another group which never sets over England is Cassiopeia, whom you will remember from the story of the princess and the sea-monster. The brightest stars in the constellation make up a W or M, and there is a simple way to find them. First, look at the second star of the Bear's tail, which has been named Mizar; you can recognize it because it has a much fainter star close beside it. Now imagine a line passing from Mizar through the Pole Star, and carried on for some way beyond. This line will lead you straight to Cassiopeia. When Cassiopeia is high up, the Bear will be low in the north; when the Bear is almost straight above your head, Cassiopeia will be low.

The Pole Star itself is in the constellation of the Little Bear, which has only one other bright star. In shape, the

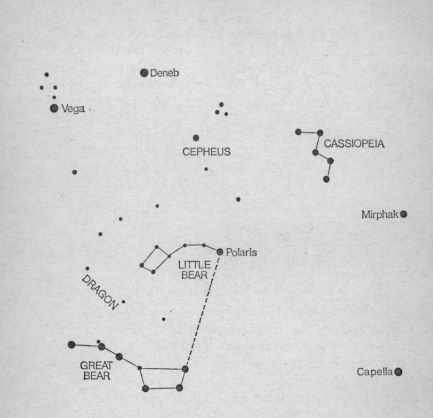

Deneb

Vega

CEPHEUS

CASSIOPEIA

Mirphak

Polaris

LITTLE
BEAR

DRAGON

GREAT
BEAR

Capella

Little Bear is not unlike the Great Bear, but it is much fainter, and if the sky is not really dark you will not see it properly.

Now let us turn to a star which is not always to be seen from England: Arcturus, which is in the constellation of the Herdsman. Arcturus is orange in colour, and very much brighter than any of the stars in the Bears or Cassiopeia. It is further away from the Pole Star, and so for part of the time it drops below the horizon. During evenings in winter, for instance, you will not see Arcturus at all. The only really important constellations which never set over England are the two Bears and Cassiopeia.

When the Bear is high up, Arcturus can be found easily by following round the 'sweep' of the Bear's tail. If you carry this line on still further, you will come to another bright star, Spica; and by using the line from the Pointers 'the wrong way' (away from the Pole Star) you will find the Lion, whose brightest star is called Regulus. All these groups are well seen during evenings in spring and early summer.

Orion, the famous hunter, is much brighter than the Bear, and you should have no trouble in finding the constellation; it is to be seen in the south from winter through to early spring. The two brightest stars are called Betelgeux and Rigel. Betelgeux (sometimes pronounced 'Beetle-juice'!) is very red; Rigel, to the bottom right of the constellation, is white. In the middle of Orion there are three rather bright stars arranged in a line. These make up the Hunter's Belt.

Follow the line of the Belt downwards, and you will come to Sirius, the brightest star in the whole sky. It too is white, but it twinkles strongly, and may even flash different colours. This is not because Sirus itself is chang-

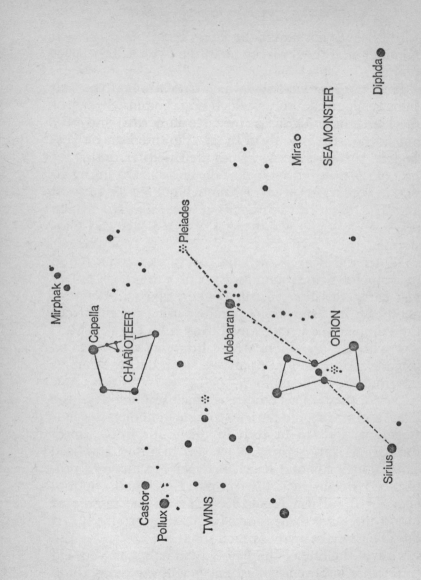

ing. A star twinkles because its light is coming to us through the Earth's air, and the air 'shakes the light about', so to speak, making the star look as if it is twinkling. A star which is low down twinkles more than a star which is high up, because its light is coming through a thicker layer of air. Sirius twinkles more than any other star, because it is so brilliant and because it never rises high in the sky as seen from Great Britain.

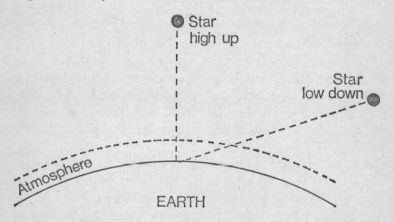

Sirius is the leader of the constellation of the Great Dog. Orion also has a smaller dog; here the brightest star is called Procyon. And not far from Procyon you can see the Twins, Castor and Pollux, whose story has already been told. Castor is not so bright as his brother – but still much brighter than the Pole Star.

Follow the Belt upwards, and you will reach another bright red star, Aldebaran – the 'Eye of the Bull'; its colour is very like that of Betelgeux. Beyond Aldebaran lies a whole cluster of fainter stars, close together; these make up the Seven Sisters, and I will say more about them later on.

High above Orion there is a very brilliant yellow star,

Capella. During winter evenings it is almost straight above you, and you cannot mistake it. It is even brighter than Rigel, though not so bright as Sirius. Close beside it you will make out a triangle of much fainter stars, which we sometimes call the Kids. Capella never sets over England, but during summer evenings it is so low down that you may not be able to find it.

If you live in the country, well away from street lights, you will also notice the Milky Way, which looks like a shining band running right across the sky, passing through Cassiopeia, near Capella, between the Twins and Orion, and down past Sirius to the southern horizon. The Milky Way is made up of stars, which are not really close together, but only seem to be so. Unfortunately, people who live in towns will not be able to see the Milky Way at all well, because it is not bright enough.

On summer evenings you will see a brilliant blue star above you; this is Vega, in the little constellation of the Harp. Two other bright stars make a large triangle with Vega; these are Deneb in the Swan and Altair in the Eagle. The Swan is sometimes called the Northern Cross, and it really is shaped like an X. Altair has a fainter star to either side of it, so that it is the middle star of a line of three. Close to the Swan and the Eagle you can find the Dolphin – which, as you will remember, carried the singer Arion safely, to the shore after he had been thrown into the sea. Both the Swan and the Eagle are crossed by the Milky Way.

Another star on view during summer evenings is Antares, in the Scorpion. The Scorpion is always low down as seen from England, but Antares is easy to find, because it is so very red and also because – like Altair – it has a fainter star to either side of it.

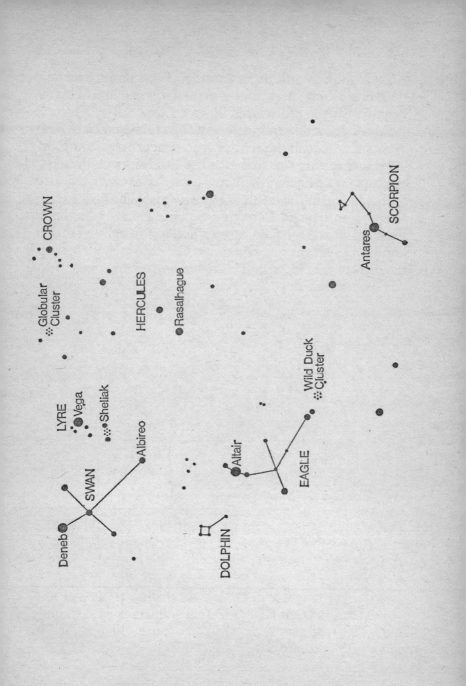

Look to the south in autumn, and you will see a constellation whose stars make up a large square. This is Pegasus. In the old stories, Pegasus was a flying horse. Leading off from it is the line of stars marking Andromeda, the princess who was so nearly gobbled up by the sea-monster; the monster itself is lower in the sky, but has no really bright stars. On the far side of Andromeda we find Perseus, the brave hero who flew to her rescue, and beyond Perseus we come back to Capella. Perseus himself is not so easy to find as some of the other groups, but if you can recognize Cassiopeia you can use the stars of the 'W' to help you, as shown here.

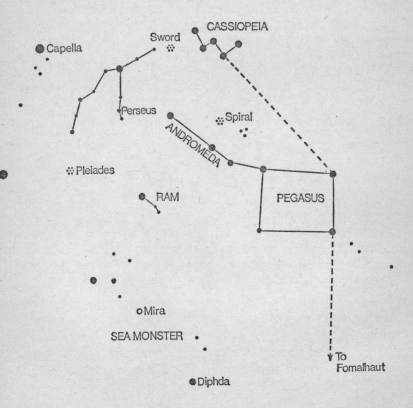

These, then, are some of the most important constellations which can be seen from Great Britain. The
following notes may help further:

WINTER EVENINGS. Orion is fairly high in the south;
Capella almost overhead; Sirius well above the southern
horizon, and all the other stars shown in the diagram on
page 26 are on view. The Great Bear is more or less
'standing on its tail' in the northern part of the sky, and
Cassiopeia is high up.

SPRING EVENINGS. The Great Bear is almost overhead;
Arcturus and Spica have come into view, and the Lion is
high in the south. Cassiopeia is now very low in the
north, and Orion has almost disappeared in the west,
though you will still be able to see Capella and the
Twins.

SUMMER EVENINGS. Vega is now almost straight above
you, and Capella is very low in the north. The Swan and
the Eagle are high, and the Scorpion, with Antares, can
be seen low in the south during evenings in early
summer. The Square of Pegasus is coming into view in
the east, but Orion cannot be seen at all.

AUTUMN EVENINGS. The Square of Pegasus is now
high in the south; Cassiopeia near the overhead point,
and the Great Bear at its very lowest in the north. Vega
is sinking in the west and Capella rising in the east. Still
further east you can already see the Seven Sisters and
Aldebaran, though Orion does not rise until well after
midnight.

If you read these notes carefully, you will soon learn
your way around the sky, but there is one thing which

you must remember. Sometimes you may see something which looks like a bright star, but which is not on your maps. This will almost certainly be a planet; and, of course, planets cannot be given on star-maps, because they move about.

A planet usually twinkles less than a star, and all the bright planets keep to the belt round the sky called the Zodiac; for instance the Twins and the Scorpion are in the Zodiac, but Orion and the Great Bear are not. Venus and Jupiter are always much more brilliant than any star (even Sirius), so that the only planets which can easily be mistaken for stars are Saturn and Mars.

5

STARS OF THE SOUTH

SO far I have been telling you about the stars which can be seen from the British Isles and the northern part of America. If you go to Australia, South Africa or New Zealand, the whole picture is different. Our Pole Star can never be seen; neither do Cassiopeia and the Great Bear show up at all well, though the Scorpion rises high in the sky, and we can see some new constellations such as the Ship and the Southern Cross. Remember, too, that the seasons are different. Christmas falls during the summer, and June is the middle of the winter. Orion can be seen just as well from Australia as from England – but it is 'the other way up', with Rigel in the top part of the constellation and Betelgeux at the bottom.

The most famous constellation in the south part of the sky is the Southern Cross. It is a very small group (in fact, it is the smallest of all the constellations), but it has some very brilliant stars. It is not really like a cross, but more like a kite! The Milky Way runs through it, and close beside it are two particularly bright stars which point towards it. Of these two, the more brilliant – known as Alpha Centauri – is the closest to us of all the bright stars. It is only a little over four light-years away, which works out to 400 thousand million kilometres.

In old stories, a Centaur was a man with a horse's body, and the constellation of the Centaur is very easy to find. It has several bright stars as well as the two which point to the Southern Cross. Look also for a path of misty light in line with two of the Cross stars. This is a star-cluster, but it is not in the least like the Seven Sisters; the stars are arranged in the form of a ball. The cluster is known as Omega Centauri.

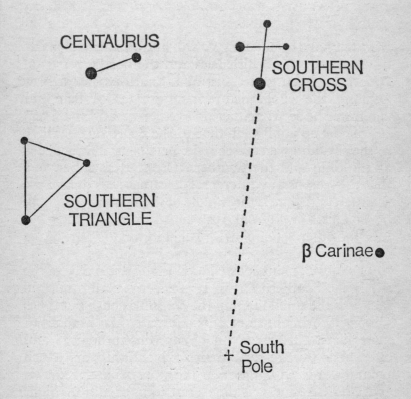

The Scorpion lies to one side of the Cross and the Centaur; from Australia and South Africa you can see it well, and its long line of stars really does make it look a little like a scorpion. On the other side of the Cross we find the Ship, which is so big a constellation that it has now been cut up into four parts. The brightest star in it is Canopus, which is more brilliant than any other star in the sky except Sirius. Canopus is much more powerful than Sirius, but it is also much further away from us. Also in the Ship we find what is called the False Cross – sometimes mistaken for the Southern Cross, though it is larger and its stars are not so bright.

There is no conspicuous star near the south pole of the sky, and the best way to find the pole is to use the Southern Cross as a guide, as shown here. Beyond the pole we come to Achernar, in the River, which is so bright that it is easy to recognize; and near Achernar are two patches of light which we call the Clouds of Magellan, because they were described by the famous explorer Magellan during his voyage round the world in 1519. The Clouds are so far away that we see them as they used to be more than 150,000 years ago; they lie outside our own star-system altogether. It is a pity that they can never be seen from England, because there are many interesting objects inside them.

Of course, many of the constellations which can be seen from Great Britain are also visible from Australia, but you must remember that they appear to be the other way around. From Australia, South Africa or New Zealand you can still use Orion as a guide, though not the Great Bear.

SUMMER EVENINGS (that is to say, around Christmas-time). Orion is in the north; Sirius is high, and Canopus almost straight above you. Achernar, too, is high up, and the Cross and the Centaur are to be found low in the south. In the north Aldebaran can be seen, and also Capella, though Capella never rises high above the horizon.

AUTUMN EVENINGS (around April). Orion is now sinking in the west, but Sirius is still in view, and Canopus remains high. The Cross is high in the south-east, together with the Centaur; the Scorpion is rising in the east. To the north the Lion may be seen; Spica is towards the east, and Achernar low in the south-west.

WINTER EVENINGS (June/July). Orion has now gone, but the Scorpion is almost overhead; it is a brilliant group, led by the red star Antares. The Cross is to the south-west; Canopus at its very lowest, in the south, so that you may have difficulty in seeing it. Arcturus has appeared in the north-west, and to the north-east you can see Vega and Altair.

SPRING EVENINGS (around October). The Square of Pegasus has now come into view in the north, while Deneb and Altair are low in the north-west, and Vega is still visible. The Scorpion is dropping in the west; Achernar is high to the south-east, but both Canopus and the Cross are low down. This is one of the best times of the year for seeing the two Clouds of Magellan. The Large Cloud is so bright that it can be seen even when the Moon is full.

It is true to say that the stars of the far south are more brilliant than those of the far north – and if you live in a country such as Australia you will always find plenty to see in the night sky.

6

HOW A STAR SHINES

WHY do the Sun and the other stars shine? If asked this question, many people will answer: 'Because they are burning.' Yet this is not true. The Sun is not burning in the same way as a fire; for one thing, it is too hot to burn in such a way!

Remember, the Sun is the only star which is close enough for us to see it really well. If it were not for the Sun, we would still know very little about the other stars. So in trying to understand what happens, let us look first at the Sun.

In *Let's Look At The Sky: The Planets* I wrote about the Sun's surface, and told you about the dark spots which are often seen on it. (I also said that is is very

dangerous to look at the Sun through any telescope, or even binoculars; if you do so, you will blind yourself for ever – so do not try it.) If we want to learn how the Sun shines, we must find out what gases are there, and for this we use a special instrument called a *spectroscope*.

Just as a telescope collects light, so a spectroscope

splits it up. What we usually call 'white' light is not really white at all, but is a mixture of all the colours of the rainbow: red, orange, yellow, green, blue and violet. The Sun's light, too, is a mixture. If a ray of sunlight is passed through a spectroscope, it is split up; and we see a coloured band, with red at one end of the band and violet at the other. We also see dark lines crossing the band, and each of these dark lines is caused by one particular kind of gas. So by looking at the Sun's 'spectrum', we can tell what gases will be found there.

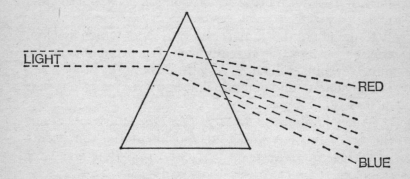

The lightest of all gases is called hydrogen. It is so light that it was once used for filling the gasbags of airships – though it can easily catch fire, so that it is no longer used in this way. Most of you will know that water is made up partly of hydrogen and partly of another gas, oxygen; in chemistry we write water as 'H_2O', showing that there are two parts of hydrogen to each part of oxygen. (Strange though it may seem, two gases put together can make liquid water!)

The Sun has a great deal of hydrogen inside it, as we can tell from its spectrum. We also know that the Sun, the heat and the pressure are so great that we cannot really picture what conditions there must be like.

Inside the Sun, the hydrogen is being changed into another kind of gas. Each time this happens, a little energy is set free, and it is this which keeps the Sun shining. We also know that as it shines, the Sun is losing weight. (We really should say 'losing mass', which is not quite the same thing; but this need not worry us for the moment.) Every second of time, the Sun is losing four million tonnes. It 'weighs' much less now than it did when you started reading this page of my book; but the Sun is so big that it will not change much for a very long time yet. It will look just the same when you have grown old as it does now.

We know that the Sun is an ordinary star; and all other ordinary stars shine in the same way – by using their hydrogen. It is easy to see that although they can go on shining for many millions of years, they cannot last for ever, because sooner or later their hydrogen will be used up. We know this because we can split up the light from other stars, just as we can do with the Sun, and tell what gases are to be found there.

From all this, you will see that the spectroscope is very important to astronomers. Without it, we would really know very little about either the Sun or the stars. In some ways a spectroscope is even more useful than a telescope – though, of course, a telescope has to be used to collect enough of the star's light for us to split up.

The Sun, then, is not in the least like a large ball of burning coal. It is shining in a very different way. A ball made of coal, burning strongly enough to send out as much light and heat as the Sun does, would burn away in less than a million years; and we know that both the Sun and the Earth are much older than that.

7

THE LIFE AND DEATH OF A STAR

IF you look up at the stars, you may think that they all look much the same, though of course some are much brighter than others. Yet this is not true. The stars are of different colours. Some of them are white, such as Sirius and Rigel; others are yellow, such as Capella – and, for that matter, the Sun; still others are red. Among the really red stars are Betelgeux in Orion and Antares in the Scorpion.

This shows us that some stars are hotter than others. One way to explain this is to heat a poker in a fire (being very careful not to burn yourself!). As it warms up, the poker starts to glow red; as it becomes hotter and hotter it turns first orange, then yellow, and then white or blue-white. In the same way, a white or blue star is hotter than a yellow star; yellow is hotter than orange, and orange is hotter than red. The surface of our yellow Sun is cooler than that of the white Sirius, but hotter than that of Betelgeux, which is red.

Some of the star-colours can be seen with the eye alone; but if you have binoculars or a telescope, you will see the colours much more clearly.

We also know that the stars are of different ages. Some have grown old, while others are still young – though remember that every star has a very long life indeed.

A star is born inside a great cloud of gas and dust in

space. There are many of these clouds; we call them *nebulæ*, and I will say more about them later. Inside a nebula, some of the dust and gas starts to collect or bunch up; a star begins to form. It shrinks, and becomes hotter inside, until at last it has become so hot that the hydrogen starts to give out energy in the way I have already explained. The star shines, and goes on doing so for as long as its hydrogen lasts.

Let us go back to the Sun, and see what will happen to it in the future. It still has plenty of hydrogen left, so that it will shine steadily for at least 5000 million years yet, but then it will run short of hydrogen, and it will change. Its inside will shrink, and its outside will swell out; the outer parts will cool down and turn red. The Sun will become a star of the kind we call a Red Giant, and for a while it will be much more powerful than it is today. Then it will shrink again, and become a very small, faint White Dwarf star.

In the sky we can see many Red Giants and many White Dwarfs. Betelgeux in Orion is a Red Giant, so that we know it to be 'old'; it has already run short of hydrogen. Because it has swelled out, it is very large, and is big enough to swallow up the whole path of the Earth round the Sun, as shown in the diagram.

Betelgeux is brilliant, because it is still sending out a great deal of energy. It is as powerful as at least three thousand Suns. A White Dwarf, on the other hand, is much smaller than the Sun, and is very dim, because it has little energy left. Sirius, the brightest star in the sky, has a small star close beside it which we know to be a White Dwarf. The White Dwarf is faint, but also very 'heavy'. If you could take a cup and fill it with material from such a star, you would find that the cup would weigh more than a large lorry.

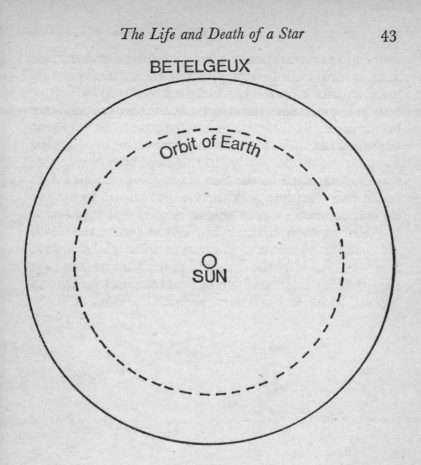

The Sun will become a White Dwarf one day. After it has become small and 'heavy', it will go on shining weakly for a long time, but at last all its light and heat will leave it, and it will end up as a cold, dark ball. There must be many of these dead stars in the sky, but we cannot see them, because they give out no light at all.

If a star begins by being much larger than the Sun, it will run through its life more quickly, and when at its brightest it will be blue-white instead of yellow. With a star which begins by being much smaller than the Sun, everything will happen much more slowly, and the star may never become a Red Giant; instead, it will simply go on shrinking until it has become a White Dwarf.

If you go out into the street, you will see babies, boys, young men and old men. You will not see a baby changing into a boy, or a boy changing into a man; everything happens much too slowly. In the same way, we cannot watch a star such as the Sun changing first into a Red Giant and then into a White Dwarf; but by looking at different stars, we can at least work out what happens.

When the Sun changes into a Red Giant, the Earth will certainly become so hot that nobody will be able to live here. Luckily, the Sun will go on shining just as it does now for many millions of years yet, so that there is no need for anyone to become worried!

8

DOUBLE STARS

THE second star in the tail of the Great Bear is named Mizar. Very close beside it is a much fainter star, known as Alcor. If your eyes are good, and the sky is clear and dark, you should be able to see Alcor easily.

Look at Mizar with a telescope, and you will see something else. Mizar itself is made up of two stars, so close together that without the telescope they appear as one. One of the Mizar pair is rather brighter than the other; Alcor is further away. Mizar, then, is a true double star, and there are plenty more double stars in the sky.

Alcor. Mizar

GREAT
BEAR

With some double stars, the two members of the pair are not really close together, but are simply lined up as seen from the Earth. One star is almost behind the other, as shown in the next diagram. Yet in most cases, the two members of a double star really are close together, and make up what we call a *binary pair*. Mizar is a binary of this kind.

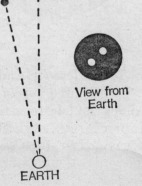

View from
Earth

EARTH

Theory of the optical double.

The boy has found the balancing-point of the dumb-bell. (See page 48)

With a binary, each star is moving round what we call the centre of gravity of the system. The best way to show what this means is to take a dumb-bell and balance it, as the boy shown on page 47 is doing. If the two bells of the dumb-bell are equal in weight, the balancing-point will be half-way between them. Now spin the pair round; each bell will move round the balancing-point, where your finger is.

With some binary stars, the two members are equal in 'weight', so that their balancing-point is half-way between them – though, of course, most binary stars are wide apart, so that each member takes months or years to go once round. But with other pairs, one member is 'heavier' than the other, and so the balancing-point lies closer to the heavier star. This is shown in the next dia-

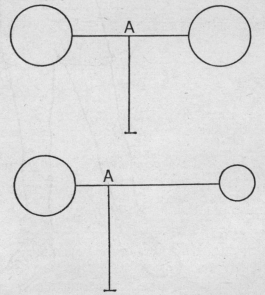

The balancing-point, A, alters position according to the relative weights of the binary stars.

gram. (If you want to prove it for yourself, fix two different weights to opposite ends of a stick, and then see where the balancing-point lies. It will always be closer to the heavier weight.)

If you have a small telescope you will be able to see many binary stars, and some of them are really beautiful. One of them is called Albireo. It lies in the constellation of the Swan, shown in the diagram on page 29; I have given the diagram again here, to show just where Albireo is. It is the faintest of the five stars of the X of the

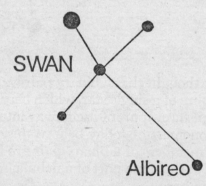

Swan. With a telescope, you will see that Albireo is a yellow star with a blue-green companion. These two suns, different in brightness and different in colour, make a lovely sight.

Another double star is Capella, which is almost overhead as seen from England during winter evenings; but the two members of the Capella pair are so close together that no ordinary telescope will show them separately. People who live in the southern part of the Earth have their double stars, too; one of them is Acrux, the leader of the Southern Cross, and another is Alpha Centauri, the nearest of the really bright stars. One member of the Alpha Centauri pair is rather more powerful than our Sun, while the other is rather fainter.

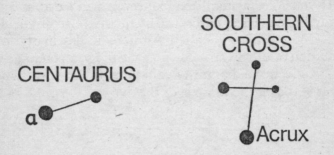

It used to be thought that a binary pair was the result of the breaking-up of a single star, which began spinning so quickly that it threw part of itself away into space, but not many astronomers of today believe this. It is more likely that the members of a binary pair are born at the same time and in the same part of a nebula, so that they always stay together.

Some stars are made up of more than two members. Castor, one of the Twins, is such a 'multiple' star. Through a telescope, it is seen to be double; we have found that each member is again double, and there is a much fainter double star not far away from the bright group. This means that Castor is made up of six suns, four of them bright and the other two dim – a sort of family party. Another of these mutiple stars lies near Vega, the brilliant blue star which is almost overhead during summer evenings as seen from England.

Suppose that we lived on a world moving round a binary star? The sky would seem very strange; there would be two suns instead of only one, and they could be of different colours.

If you have a telescope, you will enjoy looking round the night sky and finding some of these double stars. Even the Pole Star is a double – though the companion is faint, and not really easy to see.

9

STARS WHICH CHANGE IN LIGHT

MOST of the stars look the same for year after year. Our Sun has not changed much since the time when men first lived on Earth – and this is lucky for us. If the Sun became much hotter or much cooler, the Earth would become a very uncomfortable place indeed.

There are, however, some stars which change in light. These are the 'variable stars'. They are of different kinds, so let us begin with a star which is not really variable at all even though it seems to change. It is called Algol, and it lies in the constellation of Perseus.

Perseus, you will remember, was the hero who cut off the head of Medusa and used it in his rescue of the Princess Andromeda. In the sky, Medusa's head is marked by the star Algol; and the name 'Algol' really means 'Demon'. Certainly Algol, is a very strange star indeed. For most of the time it is about as bright as the Pole Star, but every two and a half days it starts to fade. For several hours it becomes dimmer and dimmer; then it stops fading, and after less than half an hour it begins to grow brighter again, until it is once more equal to the Pole Star. After this, nothing seems to happen for another two and a half days, when Algol gives another long, slow 'wink'.

The first man to find out the cause of this change was named John Goodricke. He was not an ordinary astronomer; he was only twenty years old, and he was deaf and dumb, though there was nothing the matter with his eyes. Unfortunately he died very soon afterwards.

He found that Algol is not a single star. It is a binary; that is to say it is made up of two stars, but the two members of the pair are so close together that no telescope will show them separately. Every two and half days the fainter star of the pair moves in front of the brighter one and cuts out some of the bright star's light. When the fainter star moves away, we can see the bright one again. This is why Algol seems to 'wink'. There are many other binaries of this sort in the sky, but Algol is the best-known of them.

Now let us come to the real variable stars, which are not binary pairs. The first to be discovered was a star in the constellation of the Sea-Monster (again we come back to the Perseus story!) and has been named Mira. It is at its brightest every eleven months, when it too may become as brilliant as the Pole Star; then it fades slowly, until it becomes too faint to be seen without a telescope, and it brightens up again just as slowly. Only for a few weeks in each year is it visible with the naked eye. We can usually tell how bright Mira will be at any time, because its changes are more or less regular.

Mira is a Red Giant, which means that it is an old star. It is swelling and shrinking in turn, and this is why it changes in brightness. Of course, no telescope will ever show it as more than a point of light; but we know that it is very big indeed. Mira is called a 'long-period' variable. There are many other stars like it, but all of them are fainter than Mira, because they are further away from us. The light from Mira takes just over a hundred years to reach us.

Even more interesting to astronomers are the variable

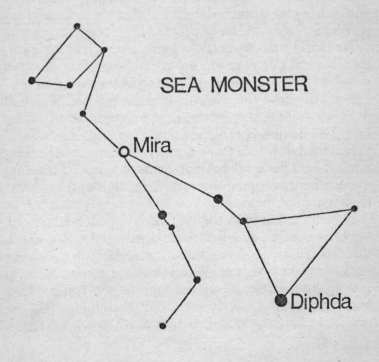

stars which change in brightness much more quickly than Mira. The best-known of these 'short-period' variables is Delta Cephei, in the constellation of Cepheus (Princess Andromeda's father), and so the variables themselves are always called Cepheids. Delta Cephei is never bright, but it can always be seen without a telescope when the sky is dark and clear. Mira, as we have seen, is at its brightest every eleven months; but Delta Cephei is at its brightest every $5\frac{1}{3}$ days. We say, therefore, that Delta Cephei has a 'period' of $5\frac{1}{3}$ days.

Cepheids are so important because as soon as we know how long they take to change in light, we can find out how far away from us they are. They are very powerful stars, much more brilliant than the Sun, and the Cepheids with the longer periods are the more powerful, so that, for instance, a Cepheid with a period of 7 days is more luminous than Delta Cephei itself, with its period of only $5\frac{1}{3}$ days. What astronomers do is to find out the period of the Cepheid, simply by looking at it, and also measuring its apparent brightness. This tells us its distance.

To explain this, imagine that you are standing on the beach looking out across the sea, and that you see a light out across the water. The light looks faint; but is it really a dim light close beside you, or a very strong light a long way away? If you know whether the light is strong or weak, you will be able to tell its distance. This is what astronomers do with the Cepheid stars. If the star looks faint, but has a long period, it must really be very powerful – and, therefore, a long way away. Because Cepheids are so much more brilliant than the Sun, we can see them even when they are many light-years from us.

Not all variable stars are like Algol, Mira or Delta

Cephei. With some of them, we can never tell what they are likely to do next. One star, in the Ship, used to shine more brightly than any star in the sky except Sirius; but for almost a hundred years now it has been too faint to be seen at all without a telescope.

10

STARS WHICH EXPLODE

SOMETIMES a brilliant star will appear in a place where no star bright enough to be seen without a telescope has ever been noticed before. This kind of star is called a *nova*. The word 'nova' means 'new', but we have found that a nova is not really a new star at all. All that happens is that a faint star explodes, and suddenly becomes bright, though after a short time – a few days, a few weeks or a few months – it fades away until it has again become very dim.

Some of these novæ have been really brilliant. One, seen in the constellation of the Eagle in the year 1918, became brighter than any star in the sky except Sirius; another, seen in 1934, became brighter than the Pole Star. Both these novæ are now so faint that you cannot see them unless you use a large telescope.

Many such stars have been seen in past years, and astronomers are very interested in them. They are old stars, which can no longer shine steadily in the way that the Sun does. However, the explosions happen in the outer parts of the star, so that the star is not blown to pieces.

It used to be thought that a nova was caused by two stars hitting each other, but we now know that this is not true. The stars are so far away from each other that they cannot often collide. There is no danger that the Sun will be hit by another star, and neither is there any danger that the Sun will turn into a nova.

Now and then there are much greater explosions, in which a star can really 'blow up', so that most of the star is sent away into space as thin gas. This is called a *super-nova*, and is quite different from an ordinary nova. Explosions of this kind do not happen very often, and it is now more than three hundred years since the last one was seen in our own star-system.

In the year 1054, before William the Conqueror came to England, a brilliant supernova appeared in the constellation of the Bull, not far from Orion. It was seen by astronomers in China, who were very surprised by it, because it became so bright that it was visible even in the daytime. After some months it slowly faded away and disappeared; of course there were no telescopes in those days, so that nobody knew what had happened to it. Hundreds of years later, when telescopes were first made, astronomers found a patch of gas in the place where the supernova had been, and there is no doubt that this gas is all that is left of the star. We call it the Crab Nebula, because a famous astronomer named Lord Rosse said that its shape looked a little like that of a crab!

You will not be able to see the Crab Nebula without a telescope, but photographs can show it well, and we know that the gas is still moving outward from the place where the old star exploded.

What about the supernova itself? It is still there, but it is no longer bright. It is very small and very 'heavy', and it is spinning round very quickly. It is called a *pulsar*, and it is sending us what are called radio waves. This is where I must say something about the new study of radio astronomy, which is not hard to understand even though it may sound rather strange.

If you throw a stone into a pond, you will set up ripples in the water. There are plenty of ripples, and the distance between the top of one ripple and the top of the next is called the 'wavelength'. Light, too, is made up of waves, but with light the wavelengths are very short. The colour of the light depends on its wavelength; blue has the shortest wavelength, and red the longest.

Now suppose that the wavelength is longer than that of red light. We cannot see the 'light' at all; it has no effect on our eyes. If the wavelength is even longer, we have radio waves.

Programmes on the wireless come to us by means of radio waves. It may sound strange to think that radio waves also come from the sky – but this is what happens, though of course the waves are not sent out by wireless stations; they are natural. Using special instruments called radio telescopes, we can study these waves; and some of them come from the pulsar in the Crab Nebula. The Sun also sends us radio waves, and so does the planet Jupiter.

A radio telescope is not in the least like an ordinary telescope, and you cannot look through it, but astronomers can learn a great deal from it. One of the largest radio telescopes in the world is shown in the next picture; it has been set up at Jodrell Bank, near Manchester, and it looks like a huge wire dish.

When a star has blown up and become a supernova, it will turn into a pulsar, and it will send us radio waves. Over a hundred of these pulsars are now known, though the pulsar in the Crab Nebula is the only one that we can see as a point of light. Without our radio telescopes, we would never have been able to find them.

These exploding stars have told us a great deal about what happens to a star when it has grown old. If the star

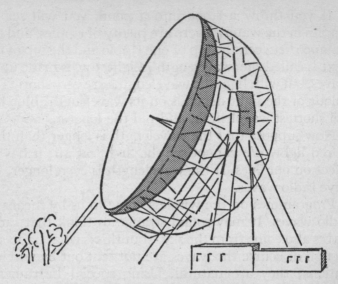

The radio telescope at Jodrell Bank.

is much larger than the Sun, it will blow up as a supernova and then become a pulsar; but the Sun itself will never do so, and after it has become a Red Giant it will simply shrink down until it becomes a White Dwarf.

If a star is so massive that it cannot become a supernova, it may go on shrinking and shrinking until not even light can get away from it, and we will not be able to see it. It will become what astronomers call a *black hole*. But we do not yet know much about these black holes, and some astronomers do not believe that they exist at all.

No supernova in our own star-system has been seen since the year 1604, but there may be another one at any time. Most of what we know about supernovæ has, therefore, been learned from watching explosions taking place in other systems of stars, so far away that their light takes millions of years to reach us.

11

CLUSTERS OF STARS

DURING winter evenings, when the sky is dark and clear, you will be able to see the lovely little group of stars which we call the Seven Sisters. They lie not very far from Aldebaran, the bright red star which marks the 'Eye of the Bull' and is in line with Orion's Belt. You cannot mistake the Seven Sisters. When you first find

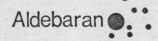

them, they may look like a misty patch; but you will soon begin to see stars in them. It is interesting to find how many stars you can see in the cluster without using a telescope or binoculars. If you can see seven, your eyes are quite good; if you can see eight or nine, your eyes are very good indeed. It is said that a German astronomer who lived a hundred years ago could see as many as nineteen stars in the group.

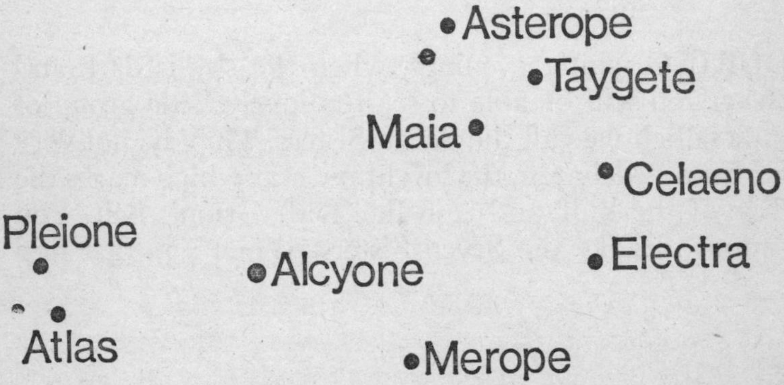

●Asterope
● ●Taygete
Maia ●

● Celaeno

Pleione
●
●Alcyone   ●Electra

● ●
Atlas   ●Merope

With a telescope or binoculars, many more stars are seen in the Seven Sisters, and altogether there are several hundred stars in the cluster. Many of them are hot and white, and much more powerful than the Sun.

The Seven Sisters make up what we call an open or loose cluster. The stars in it are much closer together than stars generally are, though even so they are so far apart that there is no danger of their hitting one another. Astronomers think that the stars in a cluster of this kind were born at about the same time, and in the same part of space.

Another cluster is called the Hyades; it is easy to find, because it lies round Aldebaran. The Hyades group is not so beautiful as the Seven Sisters, because its stars are further apart, but you will be able to make out a kind of V-shape, as shown here. Strangely enough, Aldebaran does not really belong to the Hyades at all. It lies about half-way between the cluster and the Earth, so that it appears 'in front'. The stars in the Hyades are as far away from Aldebaran as we are.

Another famous cluster, in the constellation of the Crab (not to be confused with the Crab Nebula!) is called the Beehive. It is easy to see without a telescope when the sky is dark, and binoculars show it well; from England it is visible during evenings in spring. And in the far south of the sky, in the Southern Cross, there is a cluster which is called the Jewel Box, because in it there are stars of many different colours.

Other clusters are quite different from these open groups such as the Seven Sisters or the Jewel Box. One of them lies in the constellation named after the great hero Hercules. It is easy to find if you have a pair of binoculars, and a telescope shows that the cluster is circular. We know that the stars in it are arranged in the form of a ball or globe, and so we call it a 'globular' cluster. An even brighter globular cluster is to be found in the Centaur, near the Southern Cross, but unfortunately it can never be seen from England.

A globular cluster may contain up to a million stars, and near the middle of the cluster the stars are really crowded. All the globular clusters are a very long way

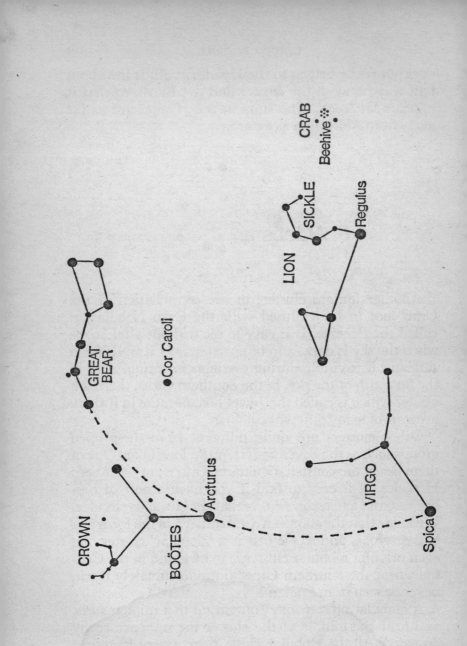

away, and are spread out round the edge of our main system.

It is not easy to measure the distances of the globular clusters, but luckily they contain the useful stars which we call Cepheid variables. As you will remember, a Cepheid changes in brightness, and the way in which it behaves tells us how powerful it is – and from this, its distance can be worked out. If we measure the distance of a Cepheid inside a globular cluster, we also know the distance of the cluster itself. Even the closest of them is so far away that its light takes more than twenty thousand years to reach us.

If we lived on a planet going round a star near the middle of a globular cluster, the night sky would be really splendid. There would be many stars bright enough to throw shadows, and there would be no darkness at all. We know that many of the brightest stars in these clusters are Red Giants, so that there would be many brilliant red stars to be seen. There may well be people living in planets moving round stars in globular clusters, though we cannot be sure.

If you have a pair of binoculars, and a star map, you will enjoy looking around the sky and finding these clusters, both open and globular. Some of them can even be seen with the naked eye, and at least you will have no trouble in find the Seven Sisters. There is an old story about this group. It was said that the Seven Sisters were girls who were once frightened by the great hunter Orion, so that they were changed into stars and taken up into the sky – where they would be safe from him!

T–C

12

CLOUDS OF GAS AND DUST

THE system of stars in which we live is called the *Galaxy*. (Remember that this is not the same thing as the Solar System, which is the Sun's family, and is made up of the Sun itself, the planets, the moons, and some less important bodies such as the comets.) There are a great many stars in the Galaxy, but the space between them is not empty. It is filled with very thin gas, and there is also 'dust', though this is not like the dust you will find in a room which has not been cleaned.

Here and there we can see clouds of gas and dust

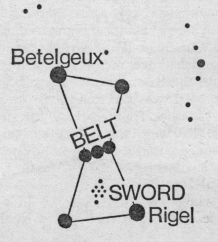

which are being lit up by stars in or near them. These clouds are called *nebulæ*, because the Latin word for 'cloud' was *nebula*. The best-known nebula is the Sword of Orion, near the three bright stars of the Belt. Without a telescope, it can be seen as a fuzzy patch; binoculars will show it well, and if you have even a small telescope you will be able to see stars there. The brightest stars in this cloud are hot and white, and it is they which make the nebula shine. Astronomers now think that there is at least one much more powerful star deep inside the nebula, but we cannot see it properly, because the nebula hides it.

The gas in a nebula is very thin indeed. It is very much thinner than the air that you breathe, and much of it is made up of the light gas hydrogen. Yet a nebula is very large, which is why we can see it so plainly.

Many other nebulæ are known, some of them easy to find with a small telescope. They are very important, because it is inside these clouds that new stars are being born. Of course, a star is not born quickly. Almost everything in the Galaxy takes a very long time indeed.

If there is no star to light up the gas and dust, the cloud will stay dark, and will be noticeable only because it will blot out the light of any star behind it. One great astronomer, who lived over a hundred years ago, thought that these starless patches were 'holes in the sky', but we now know that he was wrong. The best-marked dark patch is in the Southern Cross, and is known as the Coal Sack, because it is so black. Unfortunately it can never be seen from England, but there are other dark nebulæ in the Swan and the constellation of the Serpent-bearer.

A nebula which seems dark to us would look bright if we could see it from another place in the Galaxy.

If we look at a nebula from the Earth it seems dark, because there is no star to light it up, but if we could see it from above the cloud would appear bright – because there is a star able to light up the 'other side' of it. There is no real difference between a dark nebula and a bright one.

Not far from the brilliant blue star Vega, in the Harp, there is a nebula which is called the Ring, because it looks a little like a small, faint bicycle-tyre. Astronomers once said that it looked like a planet, and so it was called a 'planetary nebula', but we now know that the Ring is only a faint star with a large shell of gas round it. It is not really a nebula at all – and it is most certainly not a planet! Another object of the same kind, in the Great Bear, is called the Owl, because photographs taken of it really do make it look a little like an owl's face.

13

THE MILKY WAY

IF you live in the country, away from street lamps, one thing you will see at night is the Milky Way. It runs right across the sky, and it looks like a band of soft light; but it is not brilliant, and if you live in a town it is not likely that you will be able to find it. It passes through Cassippeia, the Swan, the Eagle and the Scorpion, while in the far south it goes through the Ship and the Southern Cross.

Look at the Milky Way through a telescope or a pair of binoculars, and you may have a surprise. The Milky Way is made up of stars – so many stars that you could not hope to count them. This was one of the first things to be discovered when telescopes were first made, more than three hundred and fifty years ago.

The stars in the Milky Way look as if they are touching each other, but this is not true. The stars are not crowded together, but we are seeing many of them in almost the same direction.

To show this, I must say something about the shape of the Milky Way system, which has a special name: the Galaxy. It is flattened, so that the shape is rather like that of two fried eggs clapped together back to back, as shown in the diagram (2). The Sun, with the Earth, is not in the middle of the Galaxy, but is a long way out towards the edge. In the picture, it is marked S. (In a diagram of

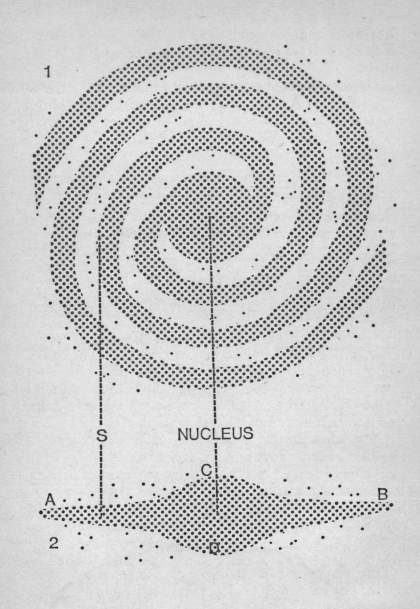

this kind, the Sun and the Earth will seem so close together that we can think of them as being in the same place.)

Now think about what will happen if we look from S toward either A or B – in fact, along the thickness of the Galaxy. We will see many stars, almost one behind the other, and this is what makes up the Milky Way. If we look 'up' or 'down' (toward C or D in the picture) we will not see nearly so many stars.

With binoculars, or a telescope, it is worth looking at different parts of the Milky Way, and seeing the crowds and crowds of stars which come into view. Summer is a good time for this – if you do not mind going to bed late! – and if you look toward the Scorpion and the Archer you will see some wonderful star-fields. The star-clouds in the Archer, a constellation next to the Scorpion, lie toward the middle of the Galaxy; but we cannot see all

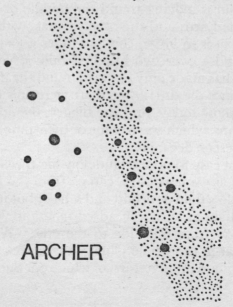

ARCHER

the way through to the middle, because there is too much 'dust' in the way. It is rather like trying to look at a far away street lamp when there is a thick fog all round you.

As well as the stars themselves, there are patches of cold, thin gas in the Galaxy, and these send out radio waves of the kind I have talked about earlier. We can find out where these cold clouds are, even though we cannot see them – they cannot be lit up by stars in the same way as nebulæ, because their gas is too thin. When we work out their positions, we find that the Galaxy is shaped like a spiral or Catherine-wheel.

Of course we cannot see the spiral shape properly, because we live inside the Galaxy; but if we could look at it from 'above' or 'below', we could see the effect plainly. We also know of other star-systems which have the same kind of shape.

The Sun is moving round the middle of the Galaxy, taking the Earth and the other planets with it. Because the Galaxy is so large, the Sun takes a long time to go once round – over two hundred million years, in fact. The Sun has made only one trip round the middle of the Galaxy since the time when there were no animals of the sort we know today, and the biggest living things were amphibians, which spent some of their time in the water and the rest on dry land.

It is not easy to understand how big the Galaxy really is. Light, as we have said, can go from the Earth to the Moon in less than a second and a half; but it would take a ray of light at least a hundred thousand years to cross the Galaxy from one side to the other. We have also found that in the whole Galaxy there are about a hundred thousand million stars, of which our Sun is only one.

14

STAR-CITIES IN SPACE

HOW far can you see without a telescope? Most people will say 'Oh – about sixteen kilometres, I suppose.' This is not the right answer. Without using any kind of telescope, or even binoculars, you can see over two million light-years, which works out at about 200 hundred thousand million million kilometres! This is the distance of the star-system which we call the Great Spiral. It is not easy to find with the naked eye, because it is not bright, but if

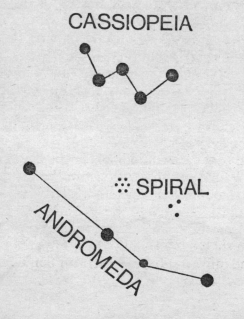

CASSIOPEIA

∴ SPIRAL

ANDROMEDA

you have good eyes you should be able to see it when the sky is dark and clear, and binoculars show it well.

We have said that our star-system or Galaxy is shaped like a spiral, and that it contains a great many stars. The Galaxy is not the only star-system. There are many others, some of them even bigger than ours; and the Great Spiral is the best-known of them. It lies in the constellation of Andromeda, near the Square of Pegasus, so that it is on view during evenings in autumn as seen from England. In it, astronomers have found some of those very useful Cepheid stars which tell us their distances, and this is how we have found out how far away the Great Spiral is.

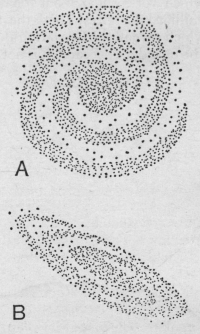

A

B

Two views of the Andromeda Spiral.

When you see it through a telescope (even a large one) it is rather disappointing, as it looks like nothing more than a foggy patch. Photographs can show us its shape, and it is a well-formed spiral (A), though it is partly edge-on to us (B), and the spiral effect is rather spoiled.

A long time ago, a French astronomer named Charles Messier drew up a list of star-clusters and nebulæ. The nebulæ seemed to be of two kinds. Some were made up of bright gas; the nebula in Orion's sword was of this kind. Others looked as if they were made up of stars. At that time nobody knew if these 'starry nebulæ' were inside our Galaxy, or were much further away. It was not until much later that astronomers were able to show that they really are outside our Galaxy altogether, so that they are separate galaxies.

Just to make sure that this is clear, let me go back for a moment. The *Solar System* is the Sun's family; it contains the Sun, the Earth and the planets. The Milky Way *Galaxy* is the star-system in which we live; the Sun is one of the many stars of the Galaxy. Far-away *galaxies* such as the Great Spiral are separate 'star-cities', well beyond the Milky Way.

Near the Great Bear, in the little constellation of the Hunting Dogs, there is another star-city, which has been called the Whirlpool because its shape is so clear. It is even further away than the Great Spiral, but it is almost face-on to us. By now thousands and thousands of galaxies are known, but not all of them are spiral. Some of them are shaped like balls, while others are quite irregular in outline.

In the south part of the sky (unfortunately, too far south to be seen from England) there are the two galaxies which we call the Clouds of Magellan. They look at first glance like broken-off parts of the Milky Way, but

each of them is more than a hundred and fifty thousand
light-years away. In the Large Cloud there is one very
powerful star which is a million times as bright as the
Sun, but because it is so far away you will have to use
binoculars or a telescope if you want to see it!

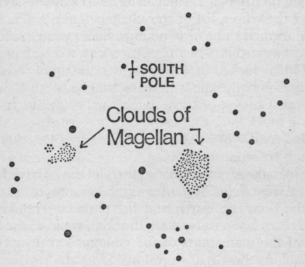

We can see stars in the nearer galaxies, such as the
Clouds of Magellan, the Great Spiral and the Whirlpool; but galaxies which are much further away look
like nothing more than tiny patches of light. It is not
easy to remember that each one of these small patches is
made up of thousands of millions of suns. In some of the
galaxies we have also seen the great explosions which we
call supernovæ, and which I had already described.
Ninety years ago a supernova was seen in the Great
Spiral, and became bright enough to be seen without a
telescope, though after a short time it faded away.

Even more interesting are the 'exploding galaxies', in which we can see great gas-clouds which we have found to be moving outward from the galaxies themselves. It seems that some tremendous explosions happened in these galaxies a very long time ago, though we do not know why. Other galaxies send us radio waves as well as ordinary light.

When we look at the galaxies, we are not seeing them as they are now. Their light takes so long to reach us that we see them as they used to be long before men lived on the Earth. Some of the galaxies are so far away that we see them as they used to be before the Earth itself was born.

With a small telescope, I am afraid that you will not see many of the galaxies; you will not be able to find the Great Spiral and, if you live in the Southern part of the world, the two Clouds of Magellan, but most of the rest are too faint to be seen unless you can use a very powerful telescope. This is not surprising when we remember how far away from us they are.

15

HOW THE GALAXIES MOVE

BECAUSE the galaxies are so far away from us, they do not seem to move at all; but astronomers have found that they are really travelling very quickly indeed. What is even more surprising is that apart from the very closest galaxies, such as the Great Spiral and the Clouds of Magellan, all of them are moving away from us; and the further away they are, the faster they are going.

To explain how this was discovered, I must say something about what we call the Doppler effect. The name comes from a scientist named Doppler, who lived in Austria many years ago.

If you listen to a car coming towards you, sounding its horn, you will hear that the note of the horn is 'high'. After the car has passed by and has begun to go further away from you, the note of the horn will become 'low'. Sound is made up of waves; and when the car is coming towards you, more sound-waves reach your ear every second than they would do if the car were standing still. The 'wavelength' is shortened, and this is why the note is high. When the car is moving away, not so many sound-waves reach your ear every second, the wavelength seems to become longer, and the note is low.

(If you live in the country, where noise cannot disturb the neighbours, ask your father to try this out! If he drives his car past you, keeping his hand on the horn, you will soon see what I mean. Of course, he will have to drive fairly fast.)

Light, as I have already told you, is made up of waves; red light has the longest wavelength and blue the shortest, so that the same kind of thing happens. When a bright object is coming towards you the wavelength will seem to be shortened, and the light will look 'too blue'; when the object is moving away, it will seem 'too red'. The change in colour is too slight to be noticed – so do not expect a red traffic-light to turn blue as you drive quickly up to it! But as we know, wc can split up the light from the stars by using spectroscopes; and from this we can tell whether the light is 'too blue' or 'too red'. If it is 'too red', then the star is moving away from us.

When this was done with the galaxies, astronomers found that all of them, beyond our own special group, were 'too red'. This meant that all the galaxies must be running away from us. For some time astronomers did not believe that this could be true, and they tried to find other ways to explain what they saw; but today almost everyone thinks that the galaxies really are moving away. If so, then the whole universe is expanding or spreading-out.

This does not mean that we live in the very middle of the universe. Every group of galaxies is moving away from every other group, just as coloured gas inside a balloon will spread out in all directions when the balloon is burst. (This is not due to the same cause, but if you can try the experiment it will help to show you what is happening.)

The furthest-away galaxies are moving at the greatest speeds, and are running away from us at the rate of thousands of kilometres every second; but they do not seem to become fainter, because they are already so distant that a few extra thousands of kilometres every second makes no difference that we can notice.

Astronomers have also found some objects which are even further away than most of the galaxies. These are called *quasars*. They look rather like foggy stars, but they are different from either stars or galaxies. Many of them send out radio waves, which is how they were first discovered, and they are very powerful indeed. A quasar is much more brilliant than a galaxy, and it looks dim only because it is so distant.

Quasars are very puzzling things. We do not know quite what they are, or why they are so powerful. Some astronomers believe that they lie inside special kinds of galaxies, but we cannot yet be sure.

Some of the quasars are further away from us than any known galaxies, so that they must be running away even faster. If a quasar (or a galaxy) is moving away at the full speed of light, we will never be able to see it at all, because its light will never reach us. Unfortunately this is something else about which we cannot yet be sure, because our telescopes cannot 'see' far enough across the universe. The more we learn, the more puzzles we find; and these strange, very powerful quasars are perhaps the most mysterious things of all.

16

HOW DID THE UNIVERSE BEGIN?

THE universe is not only very big, but also very old. It must be much older than the Earth, and also much older than the Sun. What we do not yet know is whether it has always existed, or whether it were born at one special moment in time.

Some astronomers think that the universe was born with what is often called a 'big bang'! One moment there was nothing at all; the next, the universe had begun. At first everything was crowded together, but then the gas making up the new universe started to spread out. It went on doing so, and very slowly it turned into galaxies; inside the galaxies, stars were born; and from the clouds of dust and gas moving round the stars, planets were born. Today the galaxies are still running away from each other – and if we look far enough into the future, we will come to a time when all the stars have used up their light and heat, so that the universe is dead.

I have told you that the further away from us a galaxy is, the faster it is running away, so that if it is so distant that it is moving away at the full speed of light we will never be able to see it at all. This means that there is a limit to 'how far we can see' across the universe, but it does not mean that there is nothing at all lying at a still greater distance. We do not know whether the universe has a limit, or whether space goes on and on for ever.

Other astronomers do not like the idea of the 'big bang' start, and some years ago it was suggested that the universe never had a beginning; there has always been a universe. As old stars die, fresh ones are formed from gas which appears out of nothingness. Not many people believe this now, but it is quite possible that the galaxies will not go on spreading-out until they are out of sight of each other. They may start to rush together again, until they all collide. If so, there will be a tremendous explosion, after which the whole story will begin again. There may be a 'big bang' every sixty thousand million years or so!

It is very difficult to make up our minds which of these ideas is right; and, of course, they may all be wrong. But though we cannot travel backwards in time, we can do something almost as good, because we can look at parts of the universe and see them as they used to be long ago. Remember, when we look at a galaxy which is (say) ten million light-years away, we are seeing it as it used to be ten million years ago. Some of the galaxies and quasars are much further away than this, so that we see them as they used to be before the Earth itself was born. This means that we can make up our minds whether the universe has changed much since then.

At the present moment, astronomers are still trying to find answers to a few really important questions: (1). How was the universe born? (2). Will it ever die? (3) How big is the universe? Unfortunately, we still have to admit that these questions still puzzle us. One day, we hope that we will be able to find out the truth.

17

LIFE ON OTHER WORLDS

ANOTHER question which is often asked is: 'Are there men living anywhere in space, on worlds beyond the Earth?' Once again we must admit that we cannot be sure; but most astronomers think that there is plenty of life in the universe.

Let us look first at our own home, the Sun's family or Solar System. Here we have nine planets, of which the Earth is one, together with other worlds, such as the moons and the minor planets. The Earth has thick air, which we use for breathing; there is plenty of water; and in those parts of the world where people live, it never becomes too hot or too cold. We must, then, look for another world where things are much the same.

In the Sun's family, we will find nowhere suitable. The giant planets (Jupiter, Saturn, Uranus and Neptune) have surfaces which are made up of gas which is both cold and poisonous. Mercury, the closest planet to the Sun, has no air. Venus, which comes next in order, has a very thick atmosphere, but we could not breathe it; and Venus is also very hot indeed, so that anyone going there would die at once (unless he wore a special suit to keep the heat out). Also, there is no water on Venus.

Mars is more friendly, and there is just a chance that there is some life there; but there can be no men, animals, birds, trees or flowers. The most we can expect are very low-type plants, and it is more likely that nothing at all lives on Mars. We could not breathe the planet's thin air, and there is no water, though at the poles there may be a little frost or ice.

The Moon, of course, has no life on it; we can be quite sure about this, because space-men from Earth have been there. When we build 'bases' on the Moon, as we should be able to do within the next thirty years or so, we will have to make them airtight, and all our food and water will have to be brought from Earth, together with all the air needed for breathing.

Of the moons of other planets, only one – the largest moon of Saturn, which is called Titan – is known to have a fairly thick atmosphere; but this too is made up of gas which we could not breathe, and Titan is so far from the Sun that it is very cold. It seems, then that there is no life in the Solar System except on the Earth.

Suppose that there are 'men' quite unlike ourselves, who can live on a world which is either very hot or very cold, and which has no air? This has often been suggested, but it does not seem to be possible. If it is true, than we are wrong in almost everything we believe we have found out; and not many people will think that this is so.

But even if there are no men in the Sun's family, things are very different when we come to think about the stars, many of which are very like our Sun. The Sun has a system of planets, and there is no reason why other stars, too, should not have planets of the same kind. If we could find a planet like the Earth, going round a star like the Sun, we might well expect to find life there – perhaps even men and women of the same kind as ourselves.

Our Galaxy alone contains so many stars that you could not possibly count them, and powerful telescopes can show us millions of galaxies, so that the number of stars we know to exist is unbelievably great. We cannot think that among all these stars, only the Sun has a family of planets going round it. There must be others. On far-away planets of other stars there may be astronomers who know much more about the universe than we have been able to find out as yet. Perhaps, at this very moment, they are using their telescopes to look at the Sun, and are wondering if it, too, has a planet family.

We cannot see planets of other stars, because they are too far away. Remember, a planet is much smaller than a star such as the Sun, and it has no light of its own. If we went too far away so that the Sun appeared only as a dot of light, we could have no hope of seeing the Earth close beside it. In the same way, no telescope we have yet built could possibly show a planet close to even the nearest of the stars.

Luckily, we have another way of trying to answer the question. If we have a star which is closer to us than most of the rest, and which has a large planet moving round it, the planet may pull on the star and make it 'wobble' very slowly. Of course no star can be seen to wobble; but by measuring the star's position carefully over a period of many years, astronomers thought that they might be able to find such a wobble. This is what has been done with several of the nearest stars. One of them, a faint red sun only six light-years away, is thought to have two large planets going round it, and there may be others also.

Everything that we have found out makes us believe that life is to be found all over the universe. Unfortunately we cannot yet hope to send any space-ships to the stars. We can send rockets to the Moon and planets, because they are so close to us; but it would take a space-ship millions of years to travel from the Earth to a star.

The only way in which we can hope to find out whether 'other men' exist is to listen-in to radio messages sent out by them. In America, astronomers have tried to pick up signals which could have been sent out by people living on planets moving round other stars, but they have heard nothing. Of course, radio waves travel at the same speed as light, so that everything would be out of date, if we managed to listen-in to a signal coming from a planet twenty light-years ago. We have to admit that there is very little chance of our hearing any such signal from space, though no doubt we will go on trying.

All kinds of strange stories have been written about space-ships visiting the Earth, but there is no truth in them. Astronomers do not believe in 'flying saucers' – that is to say, space-ships which have come from other worlds. Yet one day, if all goes well, we may really be able to get in touch with other intelligent beings, whether or nor they look like ourselves. This is not likely to happen in my lifetime, or in yours; but in the future we may be able to show that we are not alone in the universe.

TAKE UP ASTRONOMY!

I HOPE you have enjoyed reading this book and *Let's Look At The Sky: The Planets* book. Astronomy is a great hobby, and you too can take a real interest in it if you want to do so.

Let me, then, go back over some of the things I have said, and explain how to set about it.

First, make sure that you know what astronomy is all about – and to do this, the best thing is to read books. Once you can answer questions such as 'what is the difference between a planet and a star?' 'How does a telescope work?' and 'What causes the Milky Way?' you will be ready to read books which will take you further. Also, make sure that you go outdoors when the sky is dark, and start learning your way around the constellations. Find the Great Bear – and Orion, if it is above the horizon; use the bright groups as guides to the rest, and make some notes, so that once you have recognized a constellation you will not forget it again.

Telescopes cost a great deal of money, but there is no need to think about buying one straight away. The best thing to do is to use binoculars, which will show you the craters of the Moon, the colours of the stars, clusters and much else besides. Then, if you are still keen, start saving up for a telescope. It is also a good idea to join an astronomy club; most towns in England have them.

If you want to make astronomy your life's work, there is much that you will have to learn – and you must be very good at figures. But not many people will want to do this, and in any case you can always enjoy yourself by looking up at the sky, where there are so many wonderful things to be seen.

SOME USEFUL TERMS

ATMOSPHERE. The gas round a planet (or a star). The Earth's atmosphere is made up chiefly of two gases, oxygen and nitrogen.

BINARY STAR. A star which is really made up of two separate stars, moving round each other.

BINOCULARS. A pair of small telescopes joined together, so that you can use both eyes at once.

CEPHEID. A star which does not shine steadily, but which brightens and fades over a short period. Cepheids behave quite regularly, and by measuring how long they take to change in light we can find out how powerful they are.

CLUSTER OF STARS. A group made up of stars which are much closer together than stars usually are.

CONSTELLATION. A pattern of stars in the sky. Because the stars are not all at the same distance from us, the stars in any particular constellation need not really be close together; they simply happen to lie in the same direction as seen from the Earth.

GALAXY. The system of stars of which our Sun is a member.

GALAXIES. Other star-systems, well beyond our own. Each galaxy contains a great many stars.

HYDROGEN. The lightest of all gases. The Sun and most of the stars are made up largely of hydrogen, and water is made up of hydrogen together with oxygen.

LIGHT-YEAR. The distance travelled by a ray of light in one year. Since light moves at 186,000 miles per second, a light-year is equal to almost six million million miles.

MILKY WAY. The luminous band across the sky which is made up of many stars seen almost in the same direction. We see it when we look along the thickness of our Galaxy. See the diagram on page 70.

NEBULA. A large cloud of dust and very thin gas in space. If it is lit up by a suitable star, it seems bright.

NOVA. A very faint star which suddenly brightens up, and may become brilliant for a few days, weeks or months before fading away again.

PLANET. A body with no light of its own, moving round a star. The Sun has nine known planets, of which the Earth is one.

QUASAR. A very distant object which looks like a hazy star, but is in fact more powerful than a whole galaxy of stars.

RADIO WAVE. A 'light wave' which you cannot see, because its wavelength is too long. Radio waves are collected and studied with special instruments known as *radio telescopes*.

SATELLITE. A 'moon' – that is to say, a body moving round a planet. Our Moon is the only natural satellite of the Earth.

SOLAR SYSTEM. The Sun's family. It includes the nine planets, the satellites, and various other less important bodies as well as the Sun itself.

SPECTROSCOPE. An instrument which splits up light, and can tell us what gases exist in the body sending out the light.

STAR. A globe of hot gas, shining by its own light. The Sun is a star, and all stars are suns.

SUPERNOVA. A star which explodes, destroying itself in its old form and blowing most of its gas away into space.

TELESCOPE, REFLECTING. A telescope which collects its light by using a curved mirror.

TELESCOPE, REFRACTING. A telescope which collects its light by using a special piece of glass known as a lens (object-glass).

TWINKLING. The apparent flashing of a star, particularly when it is low down. Twinkling is caused by the Earth's air through which the starlight has to pass, and has nothing to do with the star itself.

VARIABLE STAR. A star which changes in its light from day to day.

ZODIAC. The belt round the sky in which the Sun, the Moon and the bright planets are always to be found.

SOME FAMOUS CONSTELLATIONS

ANDROMEDA. Best seen during evenings from October to January. It has some fairly bright stars, and is joined on to the Square of Pegasus. It contains the best-known of the outer galaxies, the Great Spiral.

The BULL. Best seen during evenings from October to February. Its brightest star, Aldebaran, lies in line with Orion's belt. The Bull contains the two most famous open clusters, the Seven Sisters and the Hyades, as well as the Crab Nebula.

CASSIOPEIA. A famous W of stars, always visible from England but never from New Zealand or most of Australia.

The CENTAUR. One of the brightest southern constellations, never seen from England. Its two brightest stars point to the Southern Cross.

The EAGLE. Well seen during evenings from July to November; it has one bright star, Altair, and its shape makes it easy to find. The Milky Way runs through it.

The GREAT BEAR. Sometimes called the Plough or the Big Dipper. Always visible from England; never from most of Australia or South Africa. The pattern made up by its seven chief stars cannot be mistaken.

The LION. A bright northern constellation, well seen during evenings from January to May; its leader is Regulus.

The LITTLE BEAR. Famous because it contains the Pole Star. In shape it is rather like the Great Bear, but is much fainter. The Pole Star is always visible from the northern half of the world, but is never seen from the southern hemisphere.

ORION. One of the most splendid of all the constellations; it can be seen from anywhere in the world, and is at its best during evenings from November to March. Its two brightest stars are Betelgeux and Rigel. It contains the three stars which make up the

Belt, and in the Sword there is the Great Nebula, made up of dust and gas.

PEGASUS. Best seen during evenings from October to February. Its main stars make up a square.

PERSEUS. A constellation with some fairly bright stars, next to Andromeda; Capella is on the other side of it. The most famous star in Perseus is the variable known as Algol.

The SCORPION. A brilliant group; it is made up of a curved line of bright stars, of which the most conspicuous is Antares. It is seen from England very low down during evenings in the early summer, but from Australia or South Africa it can be seen for much of the year, and may pass straight overhead.

The SHIP. A very large constellation, most of which never rises over England. Its brightest star is Canopus. It is crossed by the Milky Way.

The SOUTHERN CROSS. A small, very brilliant constellation whose outline is more like a kite than a cross. Unfortunately it is never visible from England, as it is too near the south pole of the sky.

The SWAN. Sometimes called the Northern Cross. It is well seen for much of the year from England, and is at its best during the summer, when it may pass overhead; its leading star is Deneb, and it is crossed by the Milky Way. From Australia and South Africa it is always very low down.

The TWINS. A bright constellation near Orion. The two leading stars are Castor and Pollux. The Milky Way is very rich in this part of the sky.

SOME FAMOUS STARS

Name	Constellation	Colour	Remarks
Achernar	River	White	Never seen from Europe
Acrux	Southern Cross	White	Fine binary
Albireo	Swan	Yellow	Double star; the companion is blue-green
Aldebaran	Bull	Orange-red	In line with Orion's belt. The Hyades lie round it.
Algol	Perseus	White	Variable star.
Alpha Centauri	Centaur	White	Brighter of the two pointers to the Southern Cross. Nearest bright star ($4\frac{1}{4}$ light-years away).
Altair	Eagle	White	Middle of a line of three.
Antares	Scorpion	Red	Also middle of a line of three.
Arcturus	Herdsman	Orange	In line with the Bear's tail. Very brilliant star.
Betelgeux	Orion	Orange red	Rather variable.
Canopus	Ship	White	Brighter than any star except Sirius. Not visible from England.
Capella	Charioteer	Yellow	Very bright. From England, almost overhead during winter evenings.
Castor	Twins	White	Fainter of the Twins. A multiple star.
Deneb	Swan	Yellow-ish-white	Very powerful star (equal to 10,000 Suns) but very distant, so that it looks fainter than Vega or Altair.

Mira	Sea-monster	Orange-red	Variable star.
Mizar	Great Bear	White	Naked-eye pair with Alcor. Mizar itself is double.
Pole Star	Little Bear	White	Very close to the north pole of the sky.
Pollux	Twins	Orange	Brighter Twin. Near Orion.
Procyon	Little Dog	White	Near Orion. Fairly bright.
Regulus	Lion	White	70 times more powerful than the Sun.
Rigel	Orion	White	Very powerful star – equal to perhaps 50,000 Suns. Very bright, even though it is 900 light-years away.
Sirius	Great Dog	White	Brightest star in the sky, but also one of the closest. Equal to 26 Suns. It often seems to twinkle strongly.
Spica	Virgin	White	In line with the Bear's tail and Arcturus.
Vega	Harp	Blue	Very brilliant; from England, almost overhead during evenings in summer.

TOMORROW'S WORLD Vol 2 – THE TOOLS OF 30p
CHANGE By James Burke and Raymond Baxter

552 99583 5   Carousel/Corgi

Based on the BBC T.V. programme, TOMORROW'S WORLD, this book takes a look at some of the latest developments in science and technology. Readers of all ages will find it a fascinating and stimulating book, profusely illustrated with photographs.

THE ASTRONOMY QUIZ BOOK By Patrick Moore 25p

552 54056 0   Carousel Non Fiction

Patrick Moore, well known through television coverage of Apollo moon shots has directed his talent and enthusiasm into translating mysteries of the skies into terms that we can understand. This book is full of fascinating quizzes and is expertly illustrated with easy to follow diagrams.

HOW & WHY WONDER BOOK OF FOSSILS   30p

552 86564 8

This is a comprehensive study of fossils, expertly illustrated and easy to follow. The author is an ardent naturalist and conservationist.

THE HOW AND WHY WONDER BOOK OF   30p
WORLD WAR II

552 86557 5

The second world war is already passing into history, yet it began only just over three decades ago. It is distant and remote for todays teenagers, yet the outcome of that Titanic global struggle has affected – and continues to affect – the lives of us all.

HOW AND WHY WONDER BOOKS OF   30p
OUR EARTH

552 86513 3

Despite Man's venture into outer space, the Planet Earth is still the home of all known peoples. Our Solar System may provide a planet of alternative accommodation, but most of us will continue to live on Earth. We should know as much about our planet home as we can. OUR EARTH explains how it was made and how it is changing all the time. A scientific companion to the Carousel series EVERYDAY LIFE IN PREHISTORIC TIMES.

All these books are available at your bookshop or newsagent; or can be ordered direct from the publisher. Just tick the titles you want and fill in the form below.

CAROUSEL BOOKS, Cash Sales Department, P.O. Box 11, Falmouth, Cornwall
Please send cheque or postal order, no currency.
U.K. and Eire send 15p for first book plus 5p per copy for each additional book ordered to a maximum charge of 50p to cover the cost of postage and packing.
Overseas Customers and B.F.P.O. allow 20p for first book and 10p per copy for each additional book.

NAME (Block letters) ....

ADDRESS ....

(JULY 75) ....
While every effort is made to keep prices low, it is sometimes necessary to increase prices at short notice. Corgi Books reserve the right to show new retail prices on covers which may differ from those previously advertised in the text or elsewhere.